Now I Know

Changing Seasons

Written by Rose Greydanus
Illustrated by Susan Hall

Troll Associates

Library of Congress Cataloging in Publication Data

Greydanus, Rose.
    Changing Seasons.

    (Now I know)
    Summary: Introduces the four seasons.
    1. Seasons—Juvenile literature. [1. Seasons]
I. Hall, Susan, ill. II. Title.
QH181.G73 1983   508   82-19959
ISBN 0-89375-902-3

10   9   8   7   6   5   4   3   2   1

Look at the pretty flower!

There are new plants growing in the ground.

It is spring!

The trees are covered with fat buds.

Inside, tiny leaves are growing.

The animals are busy making new homes.

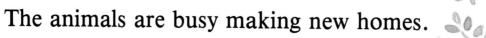

They are busy
taking care of their
new babies, too!

In spring, each day grows a little longer.

The sun is a little higher in the sky.

So, each day grows warmer and warmer.

Soon, it is summer!

Now the plants are growing strong and tall.

The sun is high up in the sky.

Summer days are long and hot.

But here's a cool spot
under a shady tree.

The baby animals are growing up.

They are learning to find their own food.

They will be ready
when the cool days
of autumn come.

Now, the days
are growing shorter.

The leaves on the trees are bright colors—
red and yellow and orange!

The sun is lower in the sky.

All the leaves have fallen to the ground.

These animals are busy looking for food.

So that when winter comes,
they won't have to leave their warm homes!

Winter days are short and cold.

Now the ground is covered with snow and ice.

Only a few animals are left.

All the rest have gone to find warmer homes.

But they will be back...

...when the days grow warmer, and spring returns!